How a Real Locomotive Works

By Bill Trombello

Illustrated by Brian Diskin

How a Real Locomotive Works

Copyright ©2010

Library of Congress Cataloging-in-Publication Data
Trombello, William,
How a Real Locomotive Works/ William Trombello
ISBN: 978-0-9842998-5-0
Juvenile

Copyright Registered: 2010
Published by Technical Training Consultants Inc. in the USA
801 Warrenville Rd.
Suite 222
Lisle, IL 60532
www.ttc-train.com
January 2010

How a Real Locomotive Works

Have you ever wondered,

"How does a real locomotive work?"

Well, climb aboard! Let's take a look...

Locomotives are big, very BIG.

A locomotive weighs about 368,000 pounds.
That's the weight of 100 automobiles.

A locomotive has a big diesel engine.
The diesel engine is the type of engine big trucks use.
The diesel engine was developed over 100 years ago
by Rudolph Diesel. The diesel engine in a
locomotive is over 18 feet long and 10 feet high!

A locomotive's diesel engine can produce 4,000 horsepower.

That's the same as 4,000 real horses all pulling together!

An automobile engine only produces about 175 horsepower.

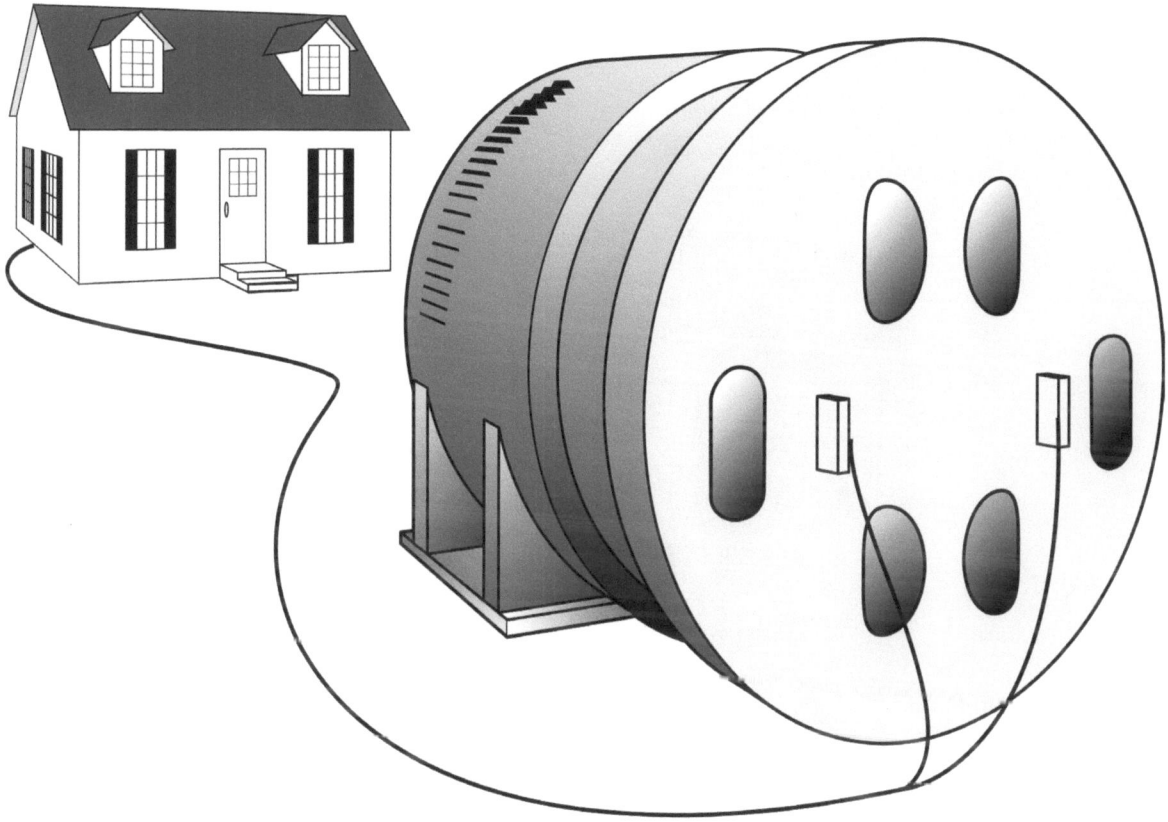

The locomotive's diesel engine is used to turn a big "Generator".

A generator produces the electricity that makes the lights . . .

the television . . .

and the computer work inside your home.

When the diesel engine turns the generator,
a locomotive's generator can produce enough
electricity to power 100 homes like yours!

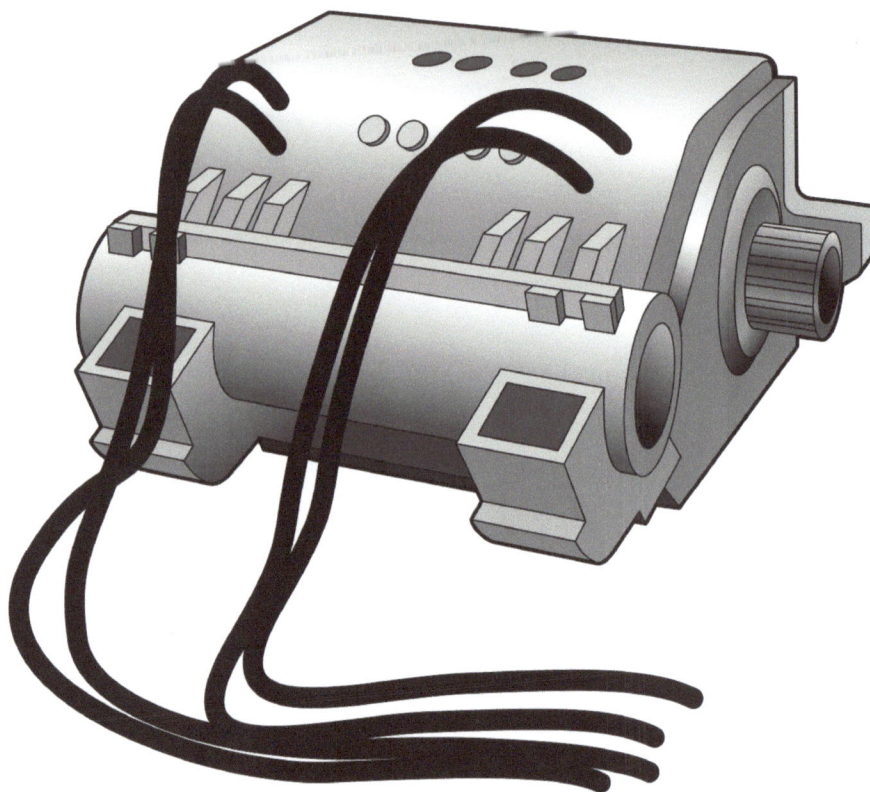

The locomotive's generator sends electricity to six electric motors called "traction motors".

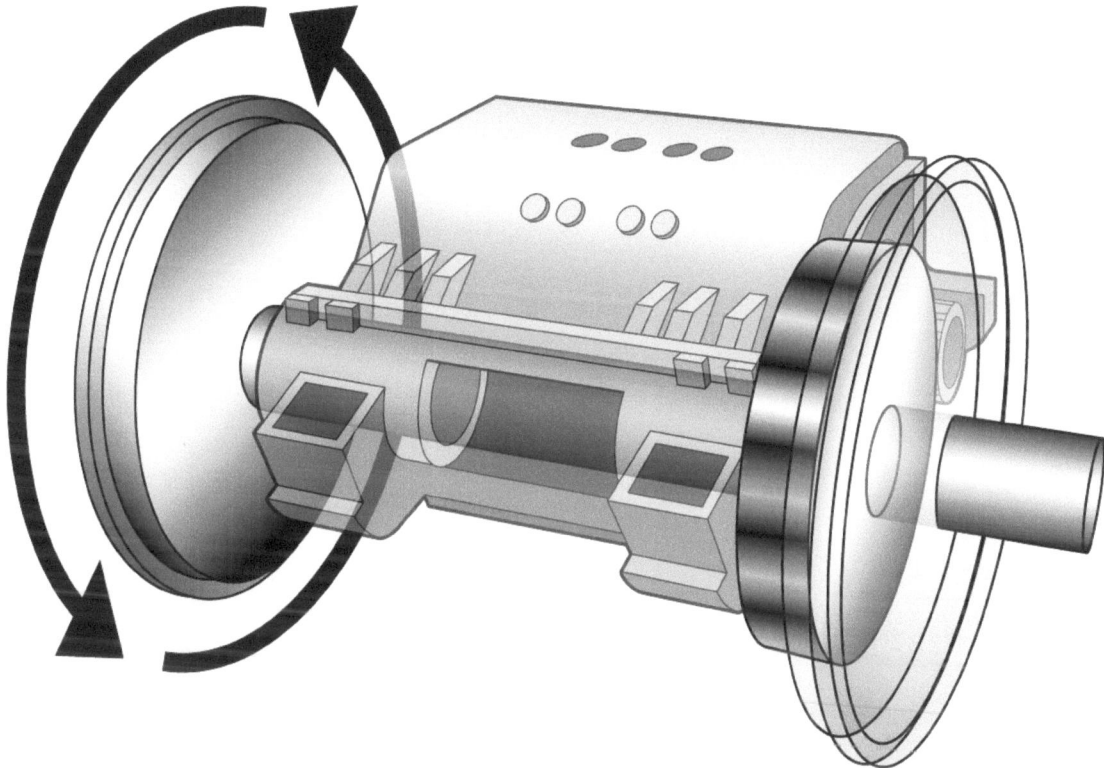

The electricity makes the traction motor's "gear" turn in a circle.

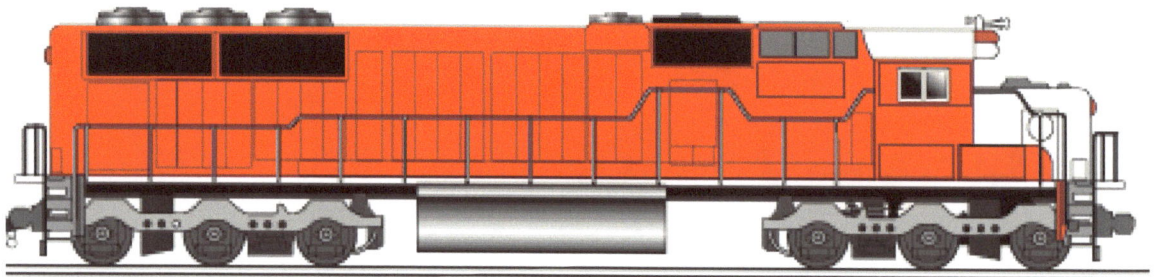

The traction motor gears turn the wheel gears that turn the wheels to make the locomotive go!

The engineer operates the locomotive from the "Cab".

The engineer uses a "reverser handle" to go forward or reverse.

The "throttle handle" is used to control how fast to go. The throttle has eight positions. Position one is the slowest speed and position eight is the fastest speed.

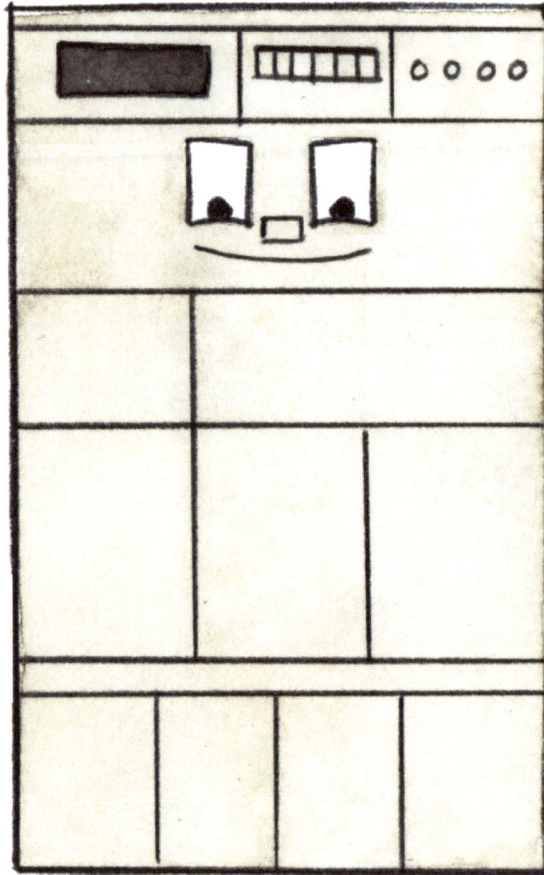

The throttle handle and the reverser handle are connected to a computer.

Let's see...
If the locomotive needs to travel 35 mph, then the generator needs 2,500 amps of electricty.

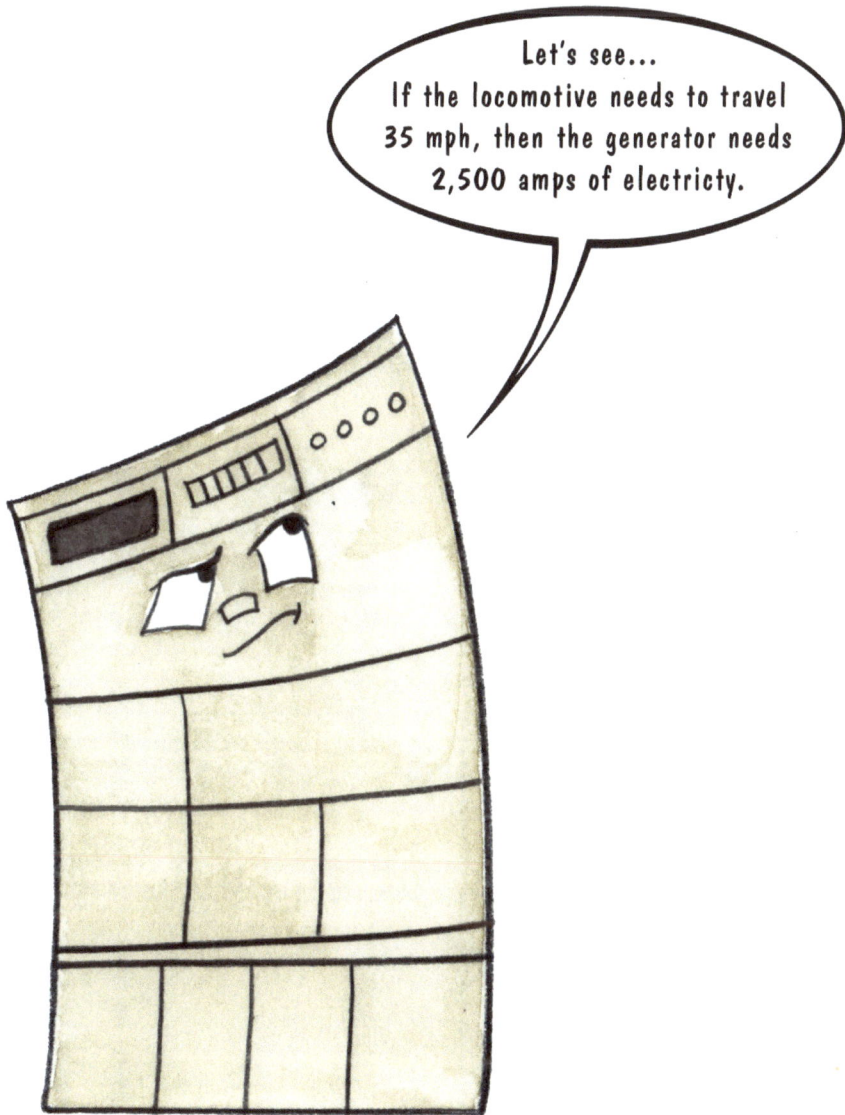

The computer decides how much electricity the generator will produce ...

When it rains or snows, the wheels on a locomotive don't grab the rails very well.

It's about the same as riding a bicycle on ice!

The tracks are slippery! I'd better reduce electricity to the traction motors.

When the railroad tracks are just too slippery for the locomotive's wheels to grab the railroad tracks, the locomotive's computer reduces power.

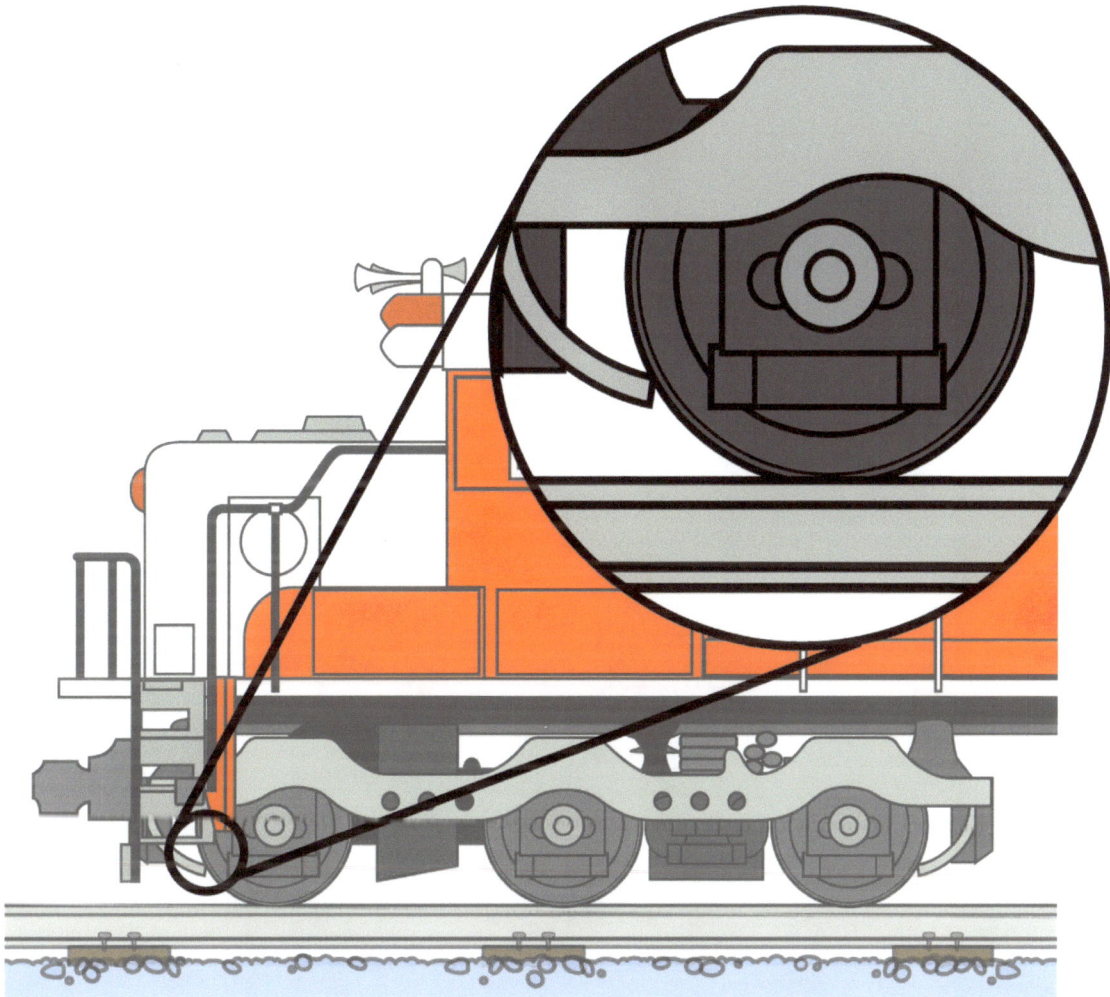

The locomotive has two sand boxes. When the tracks are slippery, the computer allows sand to drop between the wheels and rails. Sand makes the wheels grab the rails better!

To slow down or stop the train, the engineer uses the "Automatic Air Brake Handle".

Brake shoe   Brake shoe

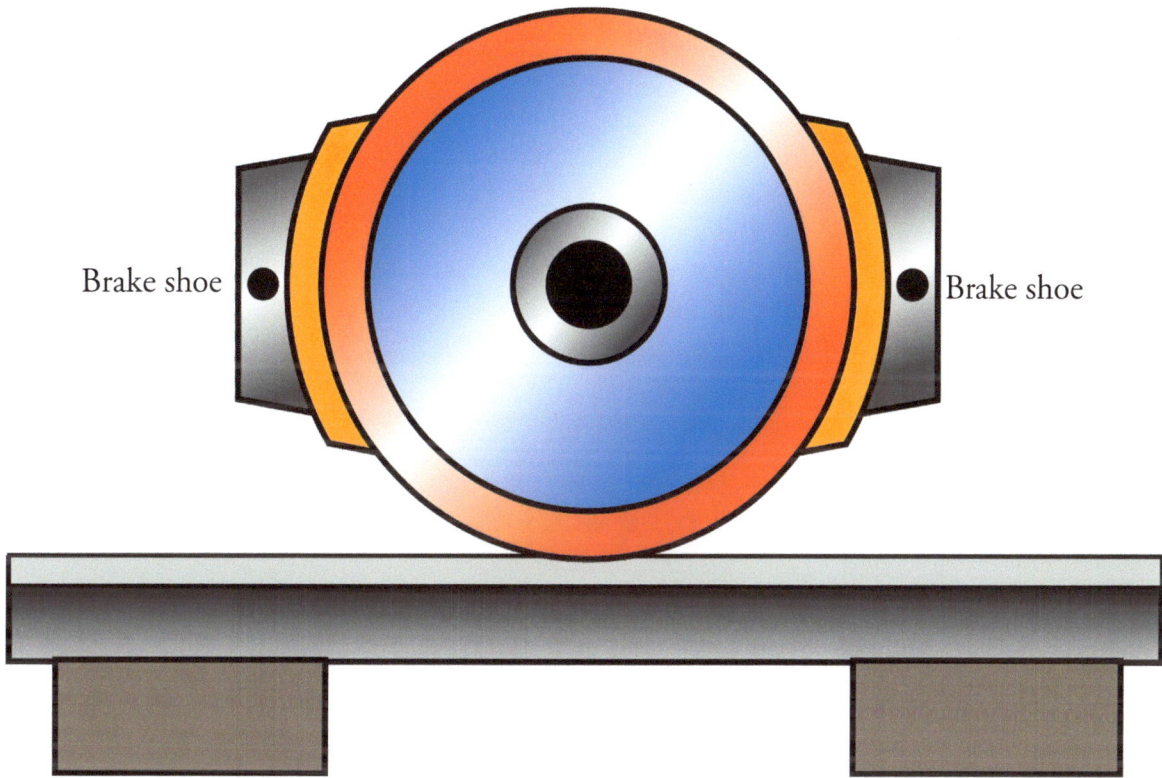

The "Automatic Air Brake Handle" applies brake shoes to the wheels on all the cars of the train.

Locomotives pull lots of heavy railroad cars.

Two locomotives can pull 100 railroad cars!

The whole train can weigh 20 million pounds!

S CREEEEECH!!! CRASH!!

Because a train is so heavy, it takes a very long time to stop!

SO, NEVER EVER TRY TO OUTRUN A TRAIN ...
by walking, riding, running or driving!

"Please, remember to be extra careful at all railroad crossings ...
Look, listen and never ever cross the railroad tracks when the gates are down!"

Also by Willaim Trombello

The Willow Falls Christmas Train

Trains and Real Locomotives

www.ingramcontent.com/pod-product-compliance
Lightning Source LLC
LaVergne TN
LVHW072122070426
835511LV00002B/62